DINOSAURS

Created and Written by
John Bonnett Wexo

Zoological Consultant
Charles R. Schroeder, D.V.M.
Director Emeritus
San Diego Zoo &
San Diego Wild Animal Park

Scientific Consultants
Edwin H. Colbert, Ph. D.
Curator Emeritus
The American Museum of Natural History
Professor Emeritus
Columbia University

John H. Ostrom, Ph. D.
Curator of Vertebrate Paleontology
Yale University

George Olshevsky, M. Sc.
Author of The Archosaurian Taxa

Creative Education

Published by Creative Education, Inc., 123 South Broad Street, Mankato, Minnesota 56001

Printed by permission of Wildlife Education, Ltd.

ISBN 0-88682-223-8

Contents

Dinosaurs are as popular with people as any living group of animals. Almost every child has been impressed by pictures of gigantic dinosaurs with long necks and tails—or frightened by pictures of dinosaurs with huge teeth, like those shown at right. At one time or another, all of us have wondered what these strange animals were really like, and what kind of weird world they might have lived in.

The word "dinosaur" means "terrible lizard." But this name is really not a good one. For one thing, dinosaurs were not very much like lizards, as you will see later on in this book. And most dinosaurs were not really terrible at all.

It's true that some of them were vicious hunters that attacked and killed other animals whenever they were hungry. But most dinosaurs were peaceful plant-eaters that rarely harmed anything except a bush or a tree.

When people want to say that something is a failure, they sometimes call it a "dinosaur." Obviously, this is because the dinosaurs died out. But the dinosaurs were not a failure at all. Before they died out, they lived on this earth for more than 160 million years—about 30 times longer than we humans have been around. The earliest dinosaurs that scientists have discovered lived more than 225 million years ago, and the last ones died about 65 million years ago. During all that time, dinosaurs dominated the world so thoroughly that the entire period was called the Age of Dinosaurs. By any standard, the dinosaurs were among the most successful animals that ever lived.

Take this dinosaur quiz. Most of us have read lots of things about dinosaurs, and seen movies about them. For this reason, we may think that we already know many facts about these "terrible lizards."

But we may not really know as much as we think we do. Because newspaper articles, popular books, and movies about dinosaurs are often filled with mistakes. Sometimes, writers and movie makers exaggerate the facts to make dinosaurs seem even bigger or more terrible. Other times, they may fail to check with scientists to find out what the real facts are.

Some of the most common errors are shown on these pages, along with the true facts.

TRUE OR FALSE?

The first people and dinosaurs lived at the same time. Cavemen and dinosaurs often fought with each other.

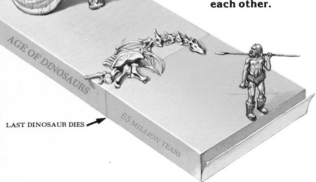

AGE OF DINOSAURS

LAST DINOSAUR DIES → 65 MILLION YEARS

ANSWER:

False. The last dinosaurs died out about 65 million years before the first people came along. No human being has ever seen a living dinosaur.

TRUE OR FALSE?

All dinosaurs were very big animals.

ANSWER:

False. The biggest dinosaurs were over 80 feet long (24 meters). But there were many smaller dinosaurs, too. The smallest was about the size of a chicken.

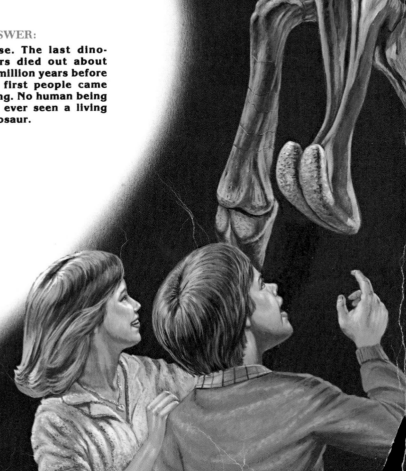

TRUE OR FALSE?

All dinosaurs had very small brains and were probably very stupid.

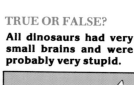

ANSWER:

False. Many dinosaurs did have small brains, but some had brains that were rather large. Scientists have found this out by measuring the areas in dinosaur skulls that would have held the brains. It is hard to judge the amount of an animal's intelligence from the size of its brain—but it seems likely that some dinosaurs were as intelligent as some modern mammals.

TRUE OR FALSE?

Dinosaurs were just like lizards and other reptiles living today, only bigger.

ANSWER:

False. Some dinosaurs were probably very different from today's reptiles. For one thing, all living reptiles are "cold-blooded." They depend on the heat in the air around them to warm their bodies so they can move. They can be active during the heat of the day ①. But they must stop moving when it gets cold at night ②.

Scientists have found evidence that some dinosaurs were "warm-blooded" like today's mammals. Mammals make heat inside their bodies, so they can move around during the day ① *and* at night ②.

There are several reasons why scientists think that some dinosaurs may have been warm-blooded. One reason has to do with dinosaur bones. Some of the bones have *canals* in them Ⓐ that are very similar to canals found in the bones of warm-blooded mammals Ⓑ. Reptiles don't have such large canals.

REPTILE BONE

Ⓑ

Ⓐ

MAMMAL BONE

CANALS

DINOSAUR BONE

TRUE OR FALSE?

All dinosaurs were clumsy and slow-moving animals.

ANSWER:

False. Big dinosaurs had a lot of weight to move around, so they probably walked slowly and carefully. But some smaller dinosaurs could probably run very fast. The fastest dinosaur may have run faster than a horse.

5 M.P.H.   10 M.P.H.   20 M.P.H.   40 M.P.H.

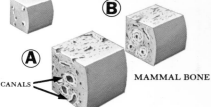

7

How do we know what dinosaurs looked like? You have probably seen many pictures of dinosaurs —but have you ever stopped to wonder how these pictures could be drawn? After all, dinosaurs died out millions of years ago, and no person ever saw one. All we have left of them is their bones.

Luckily, scientists have found ways of "reading" the bones to get some idea of the way dinosaurs looked. Starting with only a pile of bones, a scientist can make a picture of a dinosaur. This process is called *restoration* (RES-TOW-RAY-shun).

The restoration of all dinosaurs begins when scientists find their bones buried in the ground. These fossil bones have been lying in the ground for millions of years, and they are often very fragile. The scientists must take great care digging them out ①.

After they dig the bones up, the scientists send them to a museum to be studied. The bones are covered with strong plaster jackets to make sure that they aren't harmed during shipping ②. Strips of cloth are dipped into plaster and wrapped around each bone. When the plaster dries, it forms a very hard shell.

When the bones have been repaired, scientists try to see where each bone fits into the skeleton ⑤.

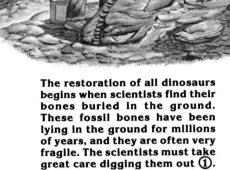

The shape of some bones can tell us how a dinosaur may have carried its body when it walked or ran.

For example, the bones in the hip of *Tyrannosaurus* have a hole in the middle Ⓐ. The ends of the leg bones were attached to the hips at this place. Above the hole, there is a sturdy ridge of bone Ⓑ.

RESTING

When *Tyrannosaurus* walked or ran, it probably held its body in a way that would keep the strong bony ridge directly over the leg bones Ⓒ. This way, the ridge would give the hip bones extra strength to take the pounding of the feet hitting the ground.

WALKING OR RUNNING

At the museum, the bones are removed from the plaster jackets and carefully repaired. Broken bones must be glued back together ③.

'd dinosaurs live? What did they
_,_ and how did they behave toward each
? did plant-eating dinosaurs protect them-
_?_ meat-eating dinosaurs? Were they good
Believe it or not, dinosaur bones and other
even tell us something about these things.
_u_ will see, scientists often study living ani-
help them understand the bodies and be-
_s_ of extinct dinosaurs. They assume that dino-
behaved in much the same way that living
als do.

_i_ course, we will never be absolutely sure that
ideas about dinosaur behavior are correct — since
ody will ever be able to check them out on living
nosaurs. But it's fun to wonder about, all the same.

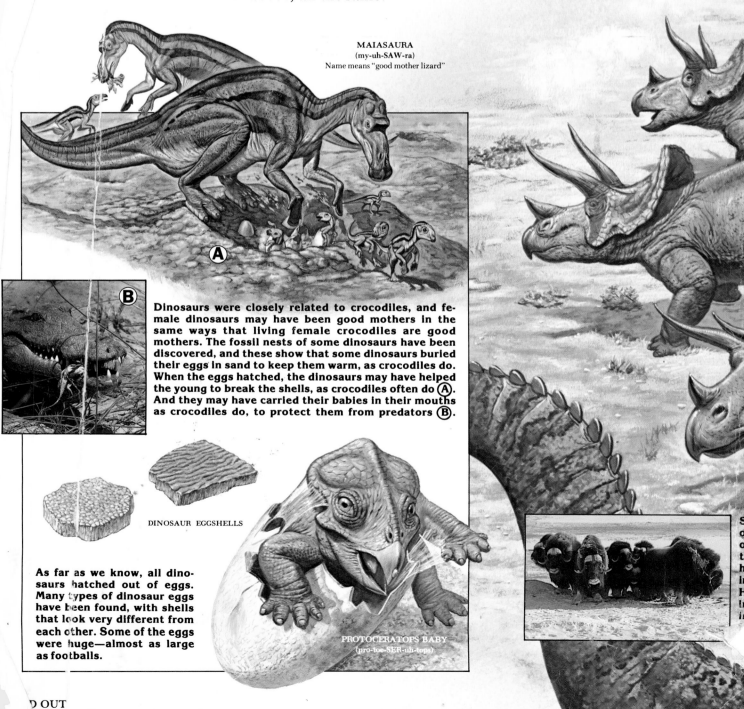

The footprints of dino-
saurs have been found
preserved in stone. And
sometimes, these fossil
footprints tell us a story
about the way dinosaurs
lived. The footprints at
right were made by a herd
of sauropod dinosaurs.

Look closely, and you will see
that the largest footprint _re on_
the outside, while the _sma_
are on the inside. This seems _t_
show that the dinosaurs kept
their young at the center of the
herd for protection as the herd
moved from place to place.

MAIASAURA
(my-uh-SAW-ra)
Name means "good mother lizard"

Dinosaurs were closely related to crocodiles, and female dinosaurs may have been good mothers in the
same ways that living female crocodiles are good
mothers. The fossil nests of some dinosaurs have been
discovered, and these show that some dinosaurs buried
their eggs in sand to keep them warm, as crocodiles do.
When the eggs hatched, the dinosaurs may have helped
the young to break the shells, as crocodiles often do (A).
And they may have carried their babies in their mouths
as crocodiles do, to protect them from predators (B).

DINOSAUR EGGSHELLS

As far as we know, all dinosaurs hatched out of eggs.
Many types of dinosaur eggs
have been found, with shells
that look very different from
each other. Some of the eggs
were huge—almost as large
as footballs.

PROTOCERATOPS BABY
(pro-toe-SER-uh-tops)

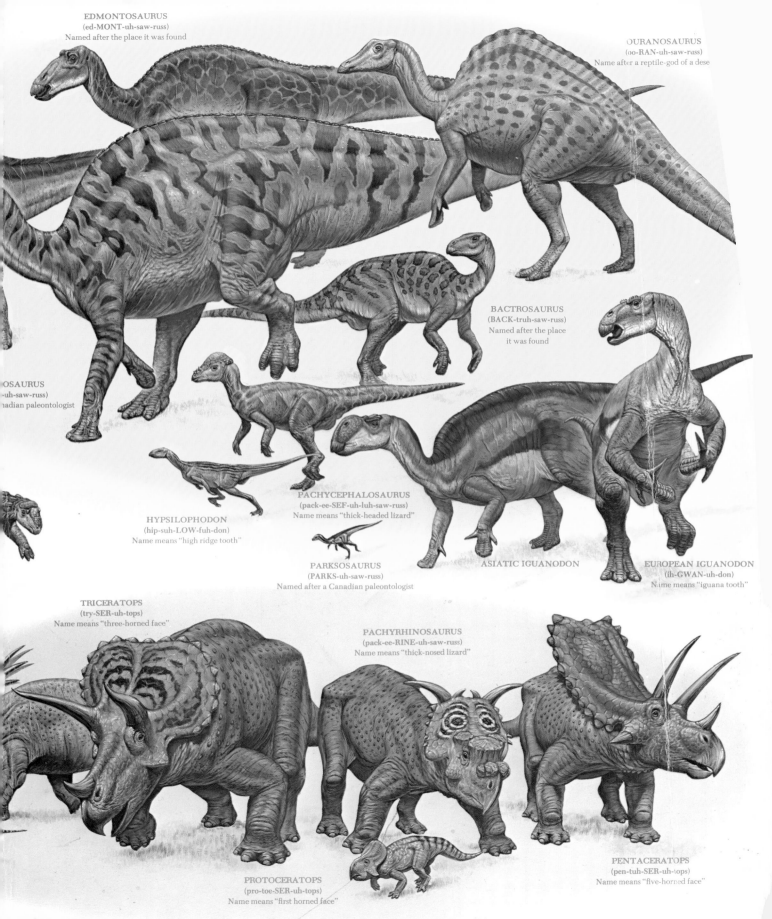

EDMONTOSAURUS
(ed-MONT-uh-saw-russ)
Named after the place it was found

OURANOSAURUS
(oo-RAN-uh-saw-russ)
Name after a reptile-god of a dese

BACTROSAURUS
(BACK-truh-saw-russ)
Named after the place
it was found

...OSAURUS
...uh-saw-russ)
...nadian paleontologist

HYPSILOPHODON
(hip-suh-LOW-fuh-don)
Name means "high ridge tooth"

PACHYCEPHALOSAURUS
(pack-ee-SEF-uh-luh-saw-russ)
Name means "thick-headed lizard"

PARKSOSAURUS
(PARKS-uh-saw-russ)
Named after a Canadian paleontologist

ASIATIC IGUANODON

EUROPEAN IGUANODON
(ih-GWAN-uh-don)
Name means "iguana tooth"

TRICERATOPS
(try-SER-uh-tops)
Name means "three-horned face"

PACHYRHINOSAURUS
(pack-ee-RINE-uh-saw-russ)
Name means "thick-nosed lizard"

PROTOCERATOPS
(pro-toe-SER-uh-tops)
Name means "first horned face"

PENTACERATOPS
(pen-tuh-SER-uh-tops)
Name means "five-horned face"

CERATOPSIANS are sometimes called the rhinoceroses of the dinosaurs. Most of them had large horns on their heads like rhinos, and very thick skin. They also probably ate many of the same kinds of food that rhinos do. But ceratopsians had huge shields on their heads that rhinos don't have. These shields were sometimes very long—more than half the length of the head in some species. The shields may have protected the neck and body when predators attacked.

1

Hundreds of different kinds of dinosaurs have been discovered. And they have been found in almost every part of the world.

As you can see on these pages, there were dinosaurs of almost any shape and size you can think of. Many had long necks and tails. Some walked on four feet while others walked on two. There were meat-eaters and plant-eaters. In general, there were dinosaurs to do most of the things that living animals do today.

Perhaps the most remarkable thing about dinosaurs is this: *only a small part* of the total number of dinosaurs that lived has probably been found. There may be thousands of new dinosaurs buried under the ground, waiting to be discovered. Somebody is going to find them. Will it be *you*?

HERRERASAURUS
(huh-RARE-uh-saw-russ)
Named after a South American paleontologist

RIOJASAURUS
(ree-OH-ha-saw-russ)
Named after the place it was found

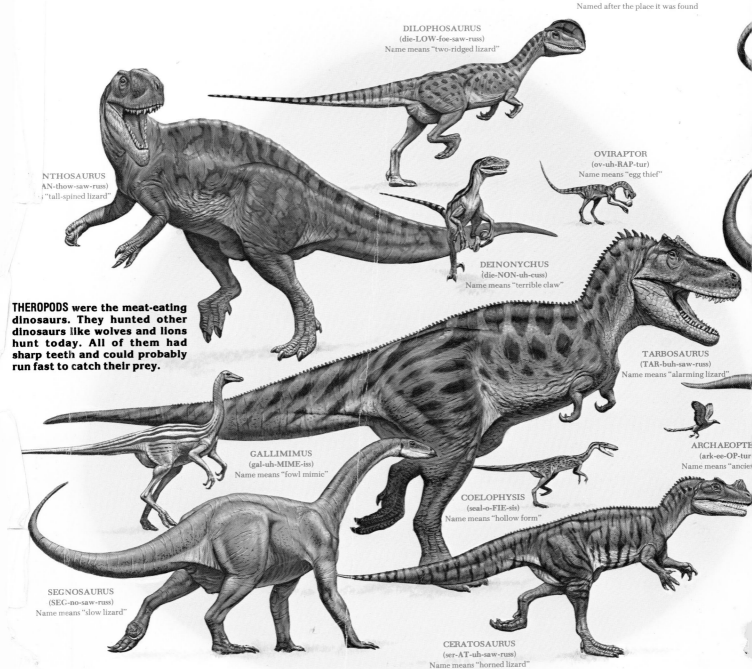

DILOPHOSAURUS
(die-LOW-foe-saw-russ)
Name means "two-ridged lizard"

OVIRAPTOR
(ov-uh-RAP-tur)
Name means "egg thief"

NTHOSAURUS
AN-thow-saw-russ)
; "tall-spined lizard"

DEINONYCHUS
(die-NON-uh-cuss)
Name means "terrible claw"

TARBOSAURUS
(TAR-buh-saw-russ)
Name means "alarming lizard"

THEROPODS were the meat-eating dinosaurs. They hunted other dinosaurs like wolves and lions hunt today. All of them had sharp teeth and could probably run fast to catch their prey.

GALLIMIMUS
(gal-uh-MIME-iss)
Name means "fowl mimic"

ARCHAEOPTE
(ark-ee-OP-tur
Name means "ancie

COELOPHYSIS
(seal-o-FIE-sis)
Name means "hollow form"

SEGNOSAURUS
(SEG-no-saw-russ)
Name means "slow lizard"

CERATOSAURUS
(ser-AT-uh-saw-russ)
Name means "horned lizard"

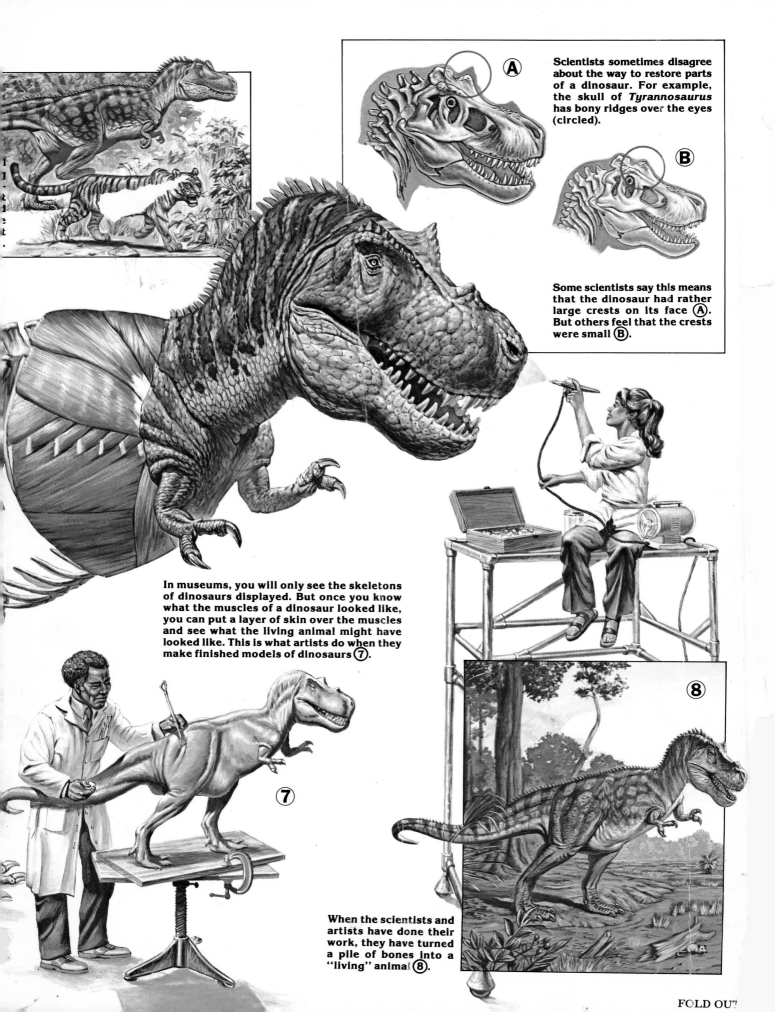

Scientists sometimes disagree about the way to restore parts of a dinosaur. For example, the skull of *Tyrannosaurus* has bony ridges over the eyes (circled).

Some scientists say this means that the dinosaur had rather large crests on its face Ⓐ. But others feel that the crests were small Ⓑ.

In museums, you will only see the skeletons of dinosaurs displayed. But once you know what the muscles of a dinosaur looked like, you can put a layer of skin over the muscles and see what the living animal might have looked like. This is what artists do when they make finished models of dinosaurs ⑦.

When the scientists and artists have done their work, they have turned a pile of bones into a "living" animal ⑧.

FOLD OUT

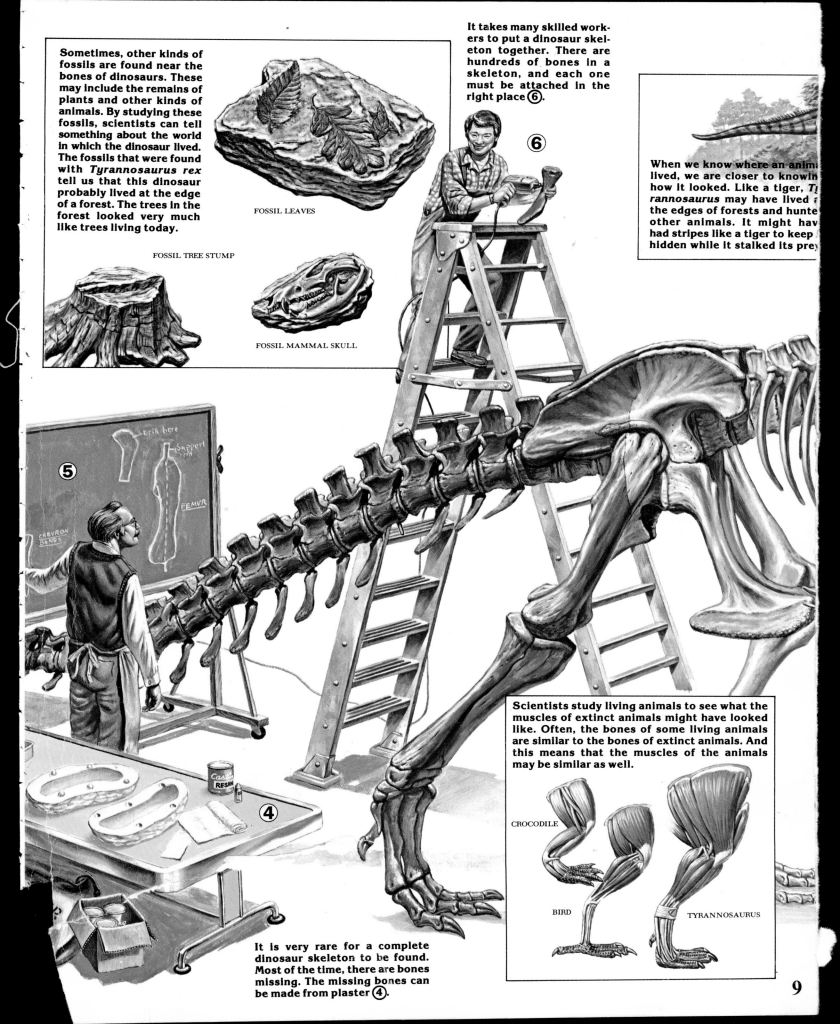

Sometimes, other kinds of fossils are found near the bones of dinosaurs. These may include the remains of plants and other kinds of animals. By studying these fossils, scientists can tell something about the world in which the dinosaur lived. The fossils that were found with *Tyrannosaurus rex* tell us that this dinosaur probably lived at the edge of a forest. The trees in the forest looked very much like trees living today.

FOSSIL LEAVES

FOSSIL TREE STUMP

FOSSIL MAMMAL SKULL

It takes many skilled workers to put a dinosaur skeleton together. There are hundreds of bones in a skeleton, and each one must be attached in the right place ⑥.

⑥

When we know where an anima lived, we are closer to knowing how it looked. Like a tiger, *Ty rannosaurus* may have lived the edges of forests and hunte other animals. It might hav had stripes like a tiger to keep hidden while it stalked its prey.

⑤

It is very rare for a complete dinosaur skeleton to be found. Most of the time, there are bones missing. The missing bones can be made from plaster ④.

Scientists study living animals to see what the muscles of extinct animals might have looked like. Often, the bones of some living animals are similar to the bones of extinct animals. And this means that the muscles of the animals may be similar as well.

CROCODILE

BIRD

TYRANNOSAURUS

PLATEOSAURUS
(PLATT-ee-uh-saw-russ)
Name means "flat lizard"

CAMARASAURUS
(cam-AIR-uh-saw-russ)
Name means "chambered lizard"

SALTASAURUS
(SALT-uh-saw-russ)
Named after the place it was found

PROSAUROPODS were some of the first dinosaurs to walk the earth. The earliest members of the group may have appeared about 225 million years ago. Most prosauropods were rather small, and usually walked on four legs. But some of them were able to rear up on two legs to run or feed.

OHMDENOSAURUS
(om-DAY-nuh-saw-russ)
Named after the place it was found

RYX
x)
t wing"

SAUROPODS were the largest of all dinosaurs. The biggest sauropod was the tallest land animal that has ever lived on earth—more than 40 feet tall (12 meters). Like giraffes, sauropods had very long necks, so they could feed on the leaves of even the tallest trees. In spite of their great size, all members of this group were peaceful plant-eaters. All of them walked on four legs, and the legs were very thick to support the tremendous weight of the animals.

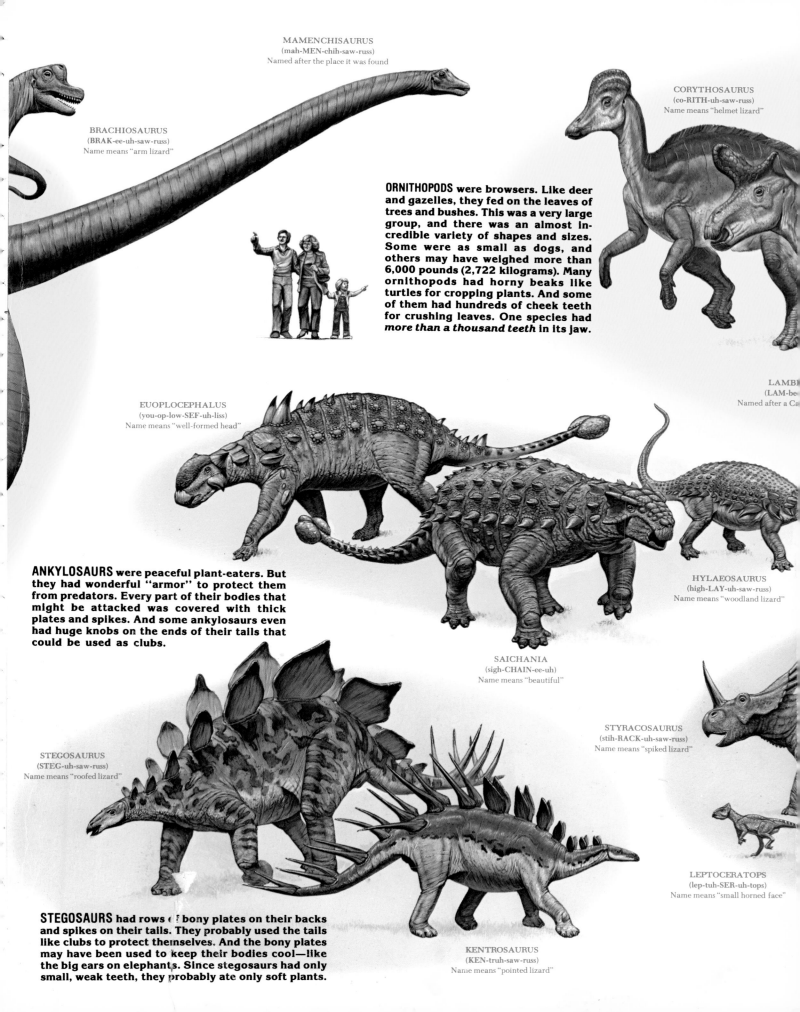

MAMENCHISAURUS
(mah-MEN-chih-saw-russ)
Named after the place it was found

BRACHIOSAURUS
(BRAK-ee-uh-saw-russ)
Name means "arm lizard"

CORYTHOSAURUS
(co-RITH-uh-saw-russ)
Name means "helmet lizard"

ORNITHOPODS were browsers. Like deer and gazelles, they fed on the leaves of trees and bushes. This was a very large group, and there was an almost incredible variety of shapes and sizes. Some were as small as dogs, and others may have weighed more than 6,000 pounds (2,722 kilograms). Many ornithopods had horny beaks like turtles for cropping plants. And some of them had hundreds of cheek teeth for crushing leaves. One species had *more than a thousand teeth* in its jaw.

LAMBI
(LAM-be
Named after a Ca

EUOPLOCEPHALUS
(you-op-low-SEF-uh-liss)
Name means "well-formed head"

HYLAEOSAURUS
(high-LAY-uh-saw-russ)
Name means "woodland lizard"

ANKYLOSAURS were peaceful plant-eaters. But they had wonderful "armor" to protect them from predators. Every part of their bodies that might be attacked was covered with thick plates and spikes. And some ankylosaurs even had huge knobs on the ends of their tails that could be used as clubs.

SAICHANIA
(sigh-CHAIN-ee-uh)
Name means "beautiful"

STYRACOSAURUS
(stih-RACK-uh-saw-russ)
Name means "spiked lizard"

STEGOSAURUS
(STEG-uh-saw-russ)
Name means "roofed lizard"

LEPTOCERATOPS
(lep-tuh-SER-uh-tops)
Name means "small horned face"

STEGOSAURS had rows of bony plates on their backs and spikes on their tails. They probably used the tails like clubs to protect themselves. And the bony plates may have been used to keep their bodies cool—like the big ears on elephants. Since stegosaurs had only small, weak teeth, they probably ate only soft plants.

KENTROSAURUS
(KEN-truh-saw-russ)
Name means "pointed lizard"

In the center of the herd, the younger dinosaurs would be safer from predators.

Like wolves and lions, some kinds of meat-eating dinosaurs probably joined together in packs to make hunting easier. A pack of wolves can catch bigger animals than a single wolf could catch. And this was probably true of dinosaurs as well.

ientists sometimes find many skeletons a single kind of plant-eating dinosaur in e place. This probably shows that some pes of plant-eating dinosaurs formed rds to protect themselves from predators, the same way that many animals do today. orned dinosaurs were probably herd an- als. And they may have used their horns the same way that musk oxen do today to nd off predators.

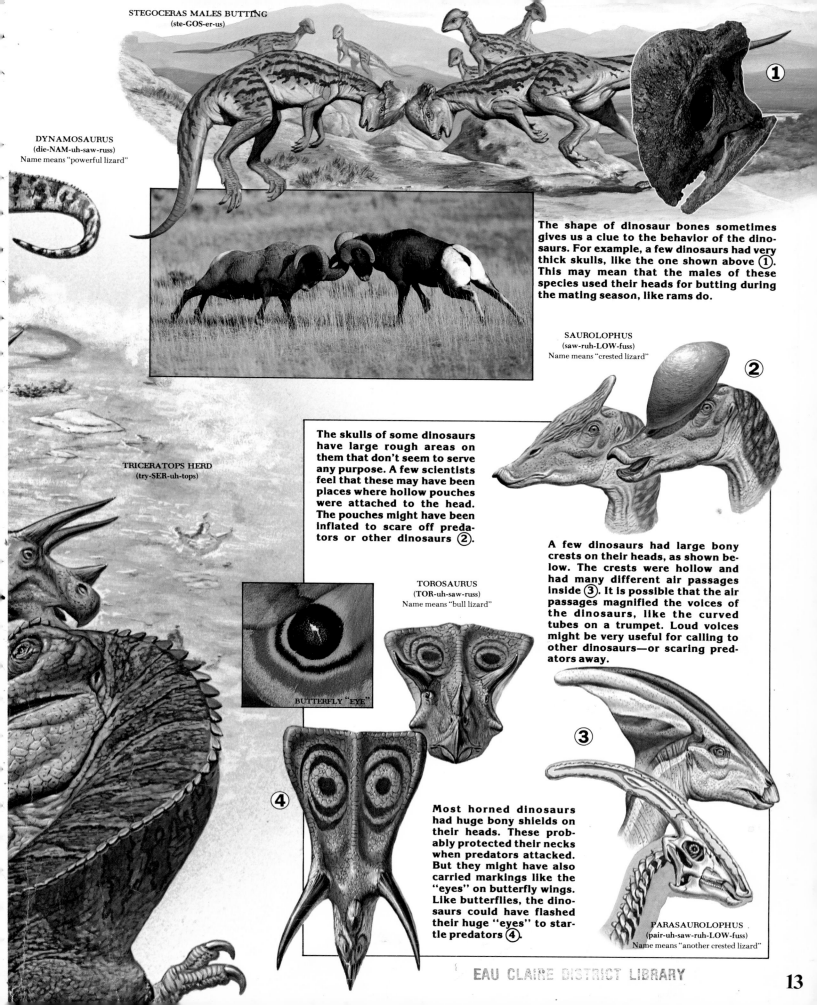

STEGOCERAS MALES BUTTING
(ste-GOS-er-us)

①

DYNAMOSAURUS
(die-NAM-uh-saw-russ)
Name means "powerful lizard"

The shape of dinosaur bones sometimes gives us a clue to the behavior of the dinosaurs. For example, a few dinosaurs had very thick skulls, like the one shown above ①. This may mean that the males of these species used their heads for butting during the mating season, like rams do.

SAUROLOPHUS
(saw-ruh-LOW-fuss)
Name means "crested lizard"

②

TRICERATOPS HERD
(try-SER-uh-tops)

The skulls of some dinosaurs have large rough areas on them that don't seem to serve any purpose. A few scientists feel that these may have been places where hollow pouches were attached to the head. The pouches might have been inflated to scare off predators or other dinosaurs ②.

A few dinosaurs had large bony crests on their heads, as shown below. The crests were hollow and had many different air passages inside ③. It is possible that the air passages magnified the voices of the dinosaurs, like the curved tubes on a trumpet. Loud voices might be very useful for calling to other dinosaurs—or scaring predators away.

TOROSAURUS
(TOR-uh-saw-russ)
Name means "bull lizard"

BUTTERFLY "EYE"

③

④

Most horned dinosaurs had huge bony shields on their heads. These probably protected their necks when predators attacked. But they might have also carried markings like the "eyes" on butterfly wings. Like butterflies, the dinosaurs could have flashed their huge "eyes" to startle predators ④.

PARASAUROLOPHUS
(pair-uh-saw-ruh-LOW-fuss)
Name means "another crested lizard"

13

How did the dinosaurs die out?

This is one of the greatest mysteries of all time, and it is still waiting to be solved. All scientists agree that the last dinosaurs died out for some reason about 65 million years ago. But they don't agree about what the reason might have been. Many different scientists have suggested many possible reasons (or *theories*), and we've shown some of the theories on these pages.

One of the most dramatic theories is based on

If the meteor landed in the ocean, it might cause a tremendous tidal wave. This monster wave would sweep ashore with great speed, and kill many dinosaurs in its path.

THEORY #2:
During the last part of the Age of Dinosaurs, new kinds of plants appeared in the world—the flowering plants. A few scientists have suggested that plant-eating dinosaurs could not digest these new plants—and starved to death as a result. Most scientists reject this theory.

THEORY #3:
A few scientists say that a strange new disease may have appeared at the end of the Age of Dinosaurs—a disease that killed only dinosaurs. Such a disease could have spread very quickly and killed all dinosaurs in a short time.

new evidence that a giant meteor from outer space may have hit the earth about 65 million years ago. If this happened, it could have caused many changes on earth that might have killed the dinosaurs.

THEORY #1:

If a huge meteor hit the earth Ⓐ, the force of the impact would probably raise millions of tons of dirt and dust into the air. It might also shake the earth enough to start eruptions from many volcanoes Ⓑ. The dense cloud of smoke and dirt in the air would keep sunlight from reaching the surface of the earth. And for this reason, most of the plants on earth would die Ⓒ.

At first, the meat-eating dinosaurs would have a feast on all the dead and dying plant-eaters. But when they had eaten all the plant-eaters, they would have no more food and would also die.

Large plant-eating dinosaurs needed large amounts of food to stay alive. If all the plants died, these dinosaurs would quickly starve to death Ⓓ. Smaller plant-eating dinosaurs might last a little longer—but they would also starve in the end.

THEORY #4:

There is a lot of evidence that there was a gradual change of the earth's climate at the end of the Age of Dinosaurs—the world got colder. Since dinosaurs were used to warmer weather, the cold could have killed them.

THEORY #5:

Mammals were very small during the Age of Dinosaurs—too small to hurt adult dinosaurs. But mammals may have eaten large numbers of dinosaur eggs, and reduced the number of dinosaurs born.

Did dinosaurs really die out?

Many scientists believe that birds are descended from one group of small dinosaurs. If this is true, then you might say that the dinosaurs didn't really die out at all. In fact, they may still be one of the most successful animal groups on earth, since there are billions of birds all over the world. Just think—the next time you see a bird, you might be looking at a living descendant of the dinosaurs!

If dinosaurs turned into birds, it took many millions of years for the process to be completed. Follow the path at right to see how it might have happened.

① SMALL DINOSAUR

DINOSAUR

The skeletons of modern birds still look like the skeletons of ancient dinosaurs in some ways. Look at the heads, necks, and legs of the dinosaur and the chicken shown here. See how similar they are.

CHICKEN

Remarkable fossils of one ancient animal have been found that seem to show a direct connection between dinosaurs and birds. This animal is called *Archaeopteryx* (ark-ee-OP-tur-ix). It may have been partly a dinosaur and partly a bird. It had teeth, a long tail, and hands with claws like a dinosaur. But it also had feathers and wings like a bird.

⑤ MODERN BIRD

Today's birds don't have teeth. But some of the earliest birds did have them. Shown above is *Hesperornis* (hess-purr-OR-nis), a bird that lived 65 million years ago. As you can see, *Hesperornis* had many small teeth that look very much like the teeth of some small dinosaurs.

There still isn't enough proof for scientists to be absolutely *sure* that living birds are relatives of the dinosaurs. But when you look at the many beautiful birds alive today, it's nice to think that the "terrible lizards" might have such wonderful descendents.

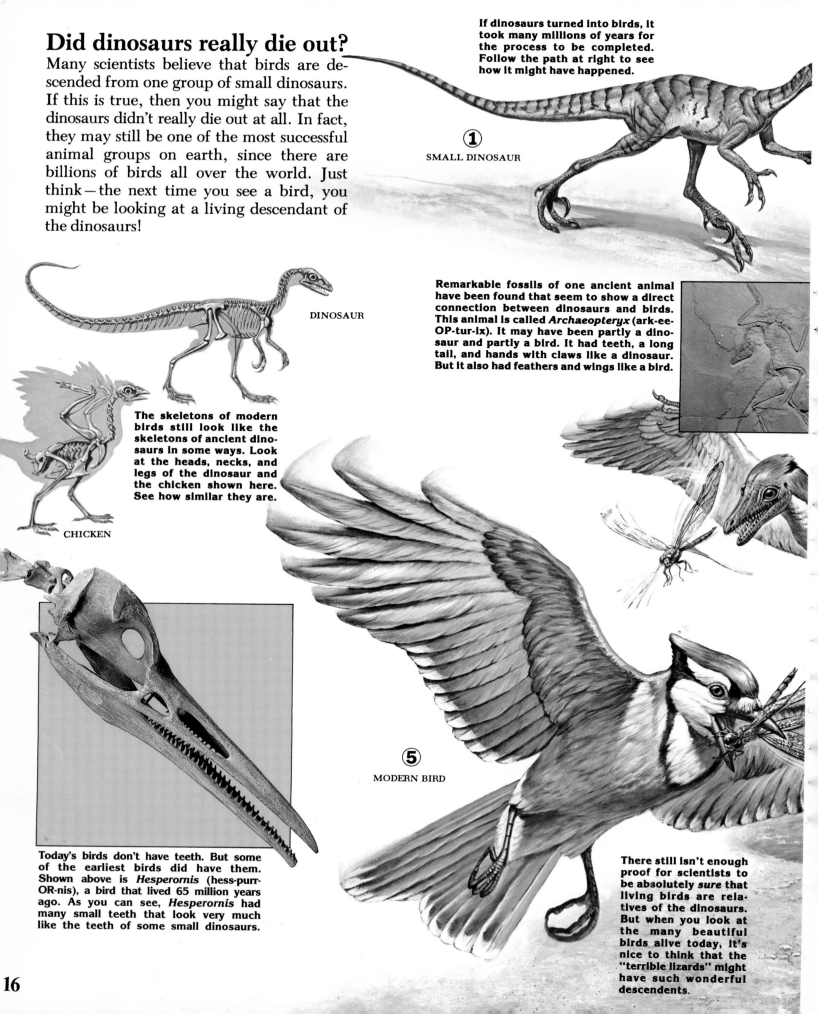

16

Millions of years ago, some small dinosaurs already looked a lot like birds. For one thing, they had feet that looked like bird feet. In fact, when the first dinosaur footprints were discovered, they looked so much like bird footprints that scientists thought they were made by giant birds.

② DINOSAUR WITH SMALL WINGS

There were small dinosaurs that had long arms. As time passed, the arms on descendents of these dinosaurs may have grown even longer and wider. If this happened, the arms would have slowly turned into wings.

③ DINOSAUR WITH FEATHERS

The structures of reptile scales and feathers are similar in certain ways. For this reason, some scientists believe that bird feathers may have developed from reptile scales. If this is true, a few types of dinosaurs may have been covered with feathers. The feathers might have helped to keep the dinosaurs warm, in the same way that bird feathers help to keep birds warm.

④ HALF DINOSAUR / HALF BIRD

Ⓐ

Ⓑ

There is a bird living today in South America that seems to show another link between birds and dinosaurs. The bird is called the *Hoatzin* (HOE-ut-sin), and scientists believe it may be the most primitive bird alive—a bird that is very similar to birds that lived millions of years ago. Like dinosaurs, baby hoatzins have claws for the first few months of their lives Ⓐ. When they grow up, they lose them Ⓑ and their wings look like the wings of other modern birds. Can you find the claws in the photograph above?

Index

Index

Art Credits

All Artwork by Mark Hallett; **Assisted by** Walter Stuart, Veronica Tagland, and Katy Vita.

Photographic Credits

Front Cover: Model by Stephen Czerkas, Photo by Chip Clark; **Page Six:** Donald Glut; **Page Twelve: Left,** Wolfgang Bayer *(Bruce Coleman, Inc.)*; **Lower Center,** J.L. Hout *(Bruce Coleman, Inc.)*; **Page Thirteen: Top Right,** Veronica Tagland; Middle, Leonard Lee Rue III (FPG); **Bottom,** E.R. Degginger *(Animals Animals)*; **Page Sixteen: Lower Left,** Mark Hallett; **Upper Right,** John Ostrom; **Page Seventeen:** Fiona Sunquist.

Our Thanks To: Steven Czerkas and Sylvia Massey-Czerkas; Dr. Walter Coombs; Dr. John McIntosh; Dr. Ralph Molnar; Dr. Wann Langston, Jr.; Dr. Robert Long *(U.C. Berkeley)*; Dr. John Harris *(L.A. County Museum of Natural History)*; Dr. Laurie MacDonald *(U.C. Berkeley)*; Dr. Hans Schultz *(University of Kansas)*; Laurie J. Bryant *(U.C. Berkeley)*; Susan Gibson *(L.A. County Museum of Natural History)*; and Lynnette Wexo.

This book is dedicated with much love to Noah John Wexo. Artwork is affectionately dedicated by the artist to Joan and John Hallett.

Creative Education would like to thank Wildlife Education. Ltd., for granting them the rights to print and distribute this hardbound edition.